CHILD WORKER

Mehboob's Story

by Catherine Chambers

Produced in association with

Plan UK

ticktock

WE WOULD LIKE TO THANK THE FOLLOWING FOR THEIR HELP IN THE PRODUCTION OF THIS BOOK:

Emma Woodgate and K. Kannan of Plan UK and Plan International (India);
Jean Coppendale and Indexing Specialists (UK) Ltd;

and our special thanks to

Mehboob

without whom this book would not have been possible.

Our thanks also goes to the International Labour Organization (ILO) for assistance in reviewing the elements of this book relevant to its work.

Copyright © ticktock Entertainment Ltd 2005
First published in Great Britain in 2005 by ticktock Media Ltd.,
Unit 2, Orchard Business Centre, North Farm Road, Tunbridge Wells, Kent TN2 3XF
ISBN 1 86007 823 0 pbk
Printed in China
A CIP catalogue record for this book is available from the British Library.

Picture credits: t=top; b=bottom; c=centre; l=left; r=right; OFC=outside front cover; OBC=outside back cover.
AFP-Getty images: 5br, 6bl, 7br, 9bl, 24, 31tr, 37tr, 41b, 42b, 43tl. Corbis: 4, 11tl 13tr, 15, 16, 20, 21t, 27bl, 28bl, 29tl, 31tl. Getty images: 5tl. Plan UK: OFC, 1, 3, 8, 10, 12, 13b, 14, 17, 18, 19, 22, 23, 25, 26, 27tr, 30, 32, 34, 35tl, 36, 38, 39, 40, 41tl, 45. ticktock archive: 21b, 33. Every effort has been made to trace the copyright holders, and we apologise in advance for any unintentional omissions. We would be pleased to insert the appropriate acknowledgements in any subsequent edition of this publication.

THE INTERVIEWER – K. KANNAN

Kannan is the Public Relations (PR) and Communications Co-Ordinator for Plan International (India). He has nearly 15 years' experience in journalism and has worked on one of India's leading newspapers, The Hindu, for over 14 years. Experienced in reporting on social issues, Kannan has been organising workshops to build bridges between the media and organisations helping families in India. As the Communications Co-Ordinator in Plan, Kannan is very interested in giving children a chance to speak out about their problems and have access to the media.

HOW MEHBOOB WAS CHOSEN

Kannan says: *"Mehboob has a deep desire and yearning to go to school, but he has a large family and his father is critically ill – so, he is forced to work. I chose Mehboob as the subject for the book because his poignant story highlights the true cost of a lost childhood, and it demonstrates the wish of many working children to continue their education. To date, all efforts to send Mehboob back to school have failed."*

THE INTERVIEW PROCESS

Kannan says: *"The interview took place in the Samuha-Plan office in the village of Irukalkada, near Hosepet. The interview took well over four hours and it was carried out in Kannada (Mehboob's language). Mehboob was very placid about the interview. There is an innocence about him that reveals the child in him, but as a working child he is already an adult. He did not find it difficult to talk about the issues in the book, but at certain points, he replied in monosyllables."*

CONTENTS

Introduction

Across the world today, over 186 million children aged between 5 and 14 are working for a living. Most do not benefit much from the wages they earn, and many do not get the chance to go to school. Without education and training, these children have few prospects for a better life in adulthood. Many child workers have to work far away from home and some never see their home or families again.

WORK CAN BE GOOD

Many young people earn money by doing a paper round or some babysitting. When they are 16, they might then take on a weekend job in a shop. Working as well as going to school gives a young person a balanced life and teaches them budgeting, work-based skills and a sense of responsibility. In most privileged societies, children and young people work in order to pay for their entertainment or luxuries – they do not have to work in order to eat. They are also protected by well-policed national and international law that stops them from being exploited as child labour.

However, working as a child or young person in many countries is not like this at all. Governments around the world and international organisations such as the International Labour Organization (ILO) and UNICEF (the United Nations Children's Fund) have put in place laws and regulations to

stop child labour. But in many countries, unscrupulous people continue to employ children and flout the law.

WHY DO CHILDREN HAVE TO WORK?

There are many reasons why children have to work. Some do it to help support their families. Others have no families at all and work to survive. UNICEF has identified some of the main reasons for child labour:

POVERTY

Most child workers have to work because their parents or carers do not earn enough money. All over the world, many adults are not paid a living wage. According to UNICEF statistics: in countries where the average yearly income for every person is US$500 or less, between 30 and 60 per cent of all children have to work.
In countries where the average yearly income for every person rises to between US$500 and 1500, between 10 and 30 per cent of all children have to work.

FINANCIAL SHOCKS

Financial 'shocks' can occur when an adult wage earner suddenly dies, or when a family member falls ill and needs healthcare that their family

This young American boy is working on his family's organic pig farm. Like many young people in developed countries, he works after school for extra allowance.

At a brick factory in Kabul, Afghanistan, children aged 7 to 11 years work from 6:30am to 4:00pm carrying wood to burn in the brick kilns.

IMPORTANT DEFINITIONS

CHILD WORK
Child work is work that does not interfere in any way with the development of children or their education. Millions of children around the world undertake work that is appropriate for their age and level of maturity and which is acceptable by law, for example, garden chores or babysitting younger brothers and sisters.

CHILD LABOUR
Child labour refers to work that is mentally, physically, socially or morally dangerous and harmful to children, or interferes with their education. It is work, therefore, that deprives children of their childhood, their potential and their dignity.

cannot afford. Around the world, the explosion of HIV and AIDS has made this situation even worse. For example, in Africa nearly 30 million people are living with AIDS or HIV. The children of AIDS sufferers have to become wage earners to support their families and pay for healthcare. At the same time they often have to farm the family plot and care for sick parents and younger siblings.

Debt is also a huge problem for poor families, and many children have to work for nothing just to pay back a family loan. Again, sometimes the loan has been incurred to cover healthcare expenses.

POOR EDUCATION AND TRAINING
Children who receive a poor education or little education often become child workers when they are very young. Whereas children who receive consistent, good-quality education are less likely to work until they reach the minimum working age, which is usually 15 or above. Well-educated children learn literacy and numeracy skills which

help them obtain better paid jobs when they are adults. They also learn self-confidence and are generally more able to detect and reject adults who can harm and exploit them.

A little girls sells pens on a street in Abidjan, Cote d'Ivoire. UNICEF's 'End of Decade' statistics showed, that in 2000, 49% of children aged 5 to 14 years in Cote d'Ivoire were working.

CHILD LABOUR IN INDIA

The problem of child labour in India is very hard to quantify, but it is believed that India has the largest number of child workers of any country in the world. UNICEF estimates that there are at least 70 to 80 million child workers in India.

In 2001, child worker statistics were gathered by the Indian government (alongside adult statistics) as part of the census. Labour statistics were broken down into three categories for various age groups (including 5 to 14 year olds): main workers (full-time workers or main wage earners), marginal workers (people who work occasionally or take part in seasonal work) and non-workers actively seeking work.

2001 CENSUS FIGURES

The number of child workers in India, according to the 2001 census, was just over 12.5 million (see table below) with an additional 4.5 million seeking or available for work.

CHILDREN AGED 5–14		
Type of worker	Number of workers	Number seeking/ available for work
Main workers	5,778,991	
Marginal	6,887,386	882,532
Non-workers	240,497,270	3,686,177

The huge difference between the census figures and UNICEF's estimates is probably due in part to the fact that India has laws against employing children under 15, especially in hazardous industries. So some parents and employers would have been reluctant to include their children and child workers in the census. Many millions of adults and children are also not officially registered in any way: for example, at a home address or place of work. This makes it impossible to take accurate census numbers. It is also worth noting that even though child employment is outlawed in India, there is nevertheless a census category for the age group 5 to 14 years called 'seeking or available for work' If a country has laws against child labour, why is there an 'available for work' statistic for such young children?

India: 10 year old Ravi cycles through Calcutta pulling a mountain of plastic bags in a small cart. Ravi contributes 25 rupees a day (35p) to his family's income by supplying plastic to the recycling industry.

REPUBLIC OF INDIA – FACTS

- *National name: Bharat*
- *Population (2004 estimate): 1,065,070,607*
- *Languages: Hindi, English and 14 other official languages*
- *Average life expectancy: 64 years*
- *Number of doctors per 100,000 people: 51*
- *Annual income per head: US$550*
- *Literacy rate (2003 estimate): male 70.2%*
                                        female 48.3%
- *Currency: Rupee (about 80 to £1 sterling)*
- *Capital city: New Delhi*
- *Geographical areas: mountainous Himalaya, flat River Ganges plain, desert south and central plateau.*

WHY CHILD WORKERS?

In India, as in many countries with a large number of child workers, there are many under-age children available for work, and it is easy to employ them very cheaply because their families are often desperate for money. Where a child's employer is their own family, it is not necessary for parents to pay their child a wage at all. Child workers are mostly too young and fearful to negotiate wages and express their rights, so employers are able to easily intimidate, manipulate and exploit them. Child workers can be made to work long hours without regular paid holidays and are offered no sick pay or compensation if they are no longer needed.

June 11, 2003: On the eve of World Day Against Child Labour a little girl sells fruit at the roadside in New Delhi, India.

EDUCATION OR WORK?

Many parents in India send their children to work instead of school. This is partly a financial decision: poor families need money, and education is not free in that parents have to pay for books and writing materials. But in addition to the cost implications, many poor families do not value education. They feel the time their child will spend at school becoming qualified for work could be better spent earning money and learning 'on-the-job skills'.

There is also a lack of confidence in education in many Indian states. There are not enough teachers, and teaching is not always of a very high standard. In rural areas, schools are often a long walk from where children live. Secondary education is also not available to all children – there are simply not enough schools.

CHAPTER ONE: Meet Mehboob

For many teenagers, going out to work is an enjoyable experience that does not interrupt their schooling. Through its Convention No.138 on the minimum age for employment, the International Labour Organization (ILO) states that 'light work' (which does not interfere with a child's education or harm their health or development) can be carried out by children aged 12 and over in developing countries.

However, around the world today, children younger than 12 are working, children aged 12 to 14 are doing more than 'light work' and children of all ages are involved in what the ILO defines as 'the worst forms of child labour'. These children are working in hazardous environments, in the armed forces or sex industry, and in slavery or forced labour. Mehboob is now 13, but he has been working since he was 8 years old.

As in the case of many child workers, Mehboob's economic situation has forced him to assume adult responsibilities while still a child.

MEHBOOB SAYS ...

"My name is Mehboob. I don't know exactly when I was born, or when my birthday is, but I am 13 years old. I was born in my village, in India. (The name of Mehboob's village has been omitted to protect his privacy.) I am a Muslim and I speak the Kannada language.

I don't know how to describe myself, about how I look, but I feel I am a good boy and I work well. I am interested in all kinds of work. I have done the work of a labourer, I've worked on road building and I've done agricultural work. I like to do the work of seed-crossing best (pollinating flowers on seed farms). And I liked going to school."

INDIA: A COUNTRY OF CONTRASTS

India's rich natural resources, such as silk, cotton and spices, made the country a target for European colonists from the 1600s onwards. By the mid-1800s, India was ruled by Britain. It became an independent country in 1947, and is now the world's largest democracy, with a globally competitive computer market and its own space programme. India is the tenth most industrialised country in the world, but not everyone in India benefits from the country's economic success, and today millions of Indian people still live in the most crushing poverty imaginable.

LOCATION OF KARNATAKA IN INDIA

Mehboob and his family live in a rural area in Karnataka state, in southwest India.

A farmer examines his parched fields. Koppal district, where Mehboob lives, suffers from drought on a regular basis.

LIFE IN THE KARNATAKA REGION

Karnataka state is divided into districts. The district where Mehboob lives is called Koppal, and, until recently, was the western part of a very large district called Raichur. Inland, Karnataka is part of India's great, rocky plateau area and the climate can be very dry, with frequent droughts. Only 9.4 per cent of Karnataka's children have normal levels of nutrition and Koppal district is one of the poorest areas in the state.

"I live with my father and mother, my four brothers and my younger sister. My older sister is called Ramzan bi, but she doesn't live with us because she got married. My father's name is Khader sab and my mother's name is Rehaman bi.

My older brother is called Raja baksh, he is 16 years old. My younger brothers are Mohammed rafi, who is 10 years old, Khan sab who is 7 years and Hussein sab who is 6 years. My youngest sister is Reshama bi, she is 3 years old.

Me, my mother and my older brother go out to work. My mother is an agricultural labourer. She has been working on a farm for the past year. She does seed-crossing. When Hussein sab was born, my mother stopped working, but she started again last year. My mother works in the house as well and prepares the food. We eat rice, jawar roti (a type of flat bread) and daal (cooked lentils with spices and onion). I have enough food to eat.

My father was working as an agricultural labourer, too. But he has been ill for the past two years. I do not know what he is suffering from – people say he has some heat (a fever). Once every month, my father goes for medical treatment at Koppal District Hospital.

Mehboob with his mother and father, two of his younger brothers and little sister, December 2004.

Madras, India: children sleep inside a cart that the family uses to collect rubbish for selling. Many children work alongside their parents to help support the family.

I feel happy when I watch the children going to school. I feel like going to school, too, but my parents are not interested in sending me there. My father is ill and not able to work. Now I must work to support the family.

What makes me angry or sad? I get angry when people use very bad and abusive language, targeting me. The older people in my village, simply to tease, use very bad language. And I feel sad when I am scolded by someone at my working place, or when difficulties come."

CHILD LABOUR AND POVERTY

The problem of child labour is directly linked to poverty – families rely on the money their children can earn in order to survive.

• Many poor families in India live in unofficial accommodation and therefore have no proper address. This means they often cannot take advantage of government aid programmes, such as food subsidies that are given out through the Public Distribution System (PDS).

• Many families who live in rural parts of India have no land of their own on which to grow food. As a result, they have to buy all the food they need. Some rural families have had to sell or give away their land to pay up debts.

• Most poor people in India who do own land, only have about 2.5 acres (1 hectare). Their only irrigation is rain, so during times of drought, their crops fail forcing them to spend the little money they do have on food.

• Rural farming families in India often receive very low prices for their cash crops, such as cotton and coffee. To make their farms viable, they use their own children as free labour.

CHAPTER TWO: My Life

Today, 330 million people in India live below the official poverty line. For children like Mehboob a childhood spent studying and playing with friends is simply not an option. His parents cannot manage without his wages and, while he is protected by law from having to work, the needs of his family override his rights to be a child.

MEHBOOB SAYS ...

"I love my home. It has a roof of tin sheets. There are two rooms. In one of the rooms my mother and father sleep. The other room is the kitchen. All the children, including me, sleep outside of the house.

We do not have running water in our house, but we bring it from the village tank. I go, or my younger brother goes, to bring the water. I also help to clean the house and I go to the shop to buy whatever mother asks of me. I have a radio, but no television.

Mehboob and his brothers and sisters sleep at the side of the house. They do not have beds.

We have some land where we grow jawar (a millet crop), groundnut and sunflowers (for seeds). We keep some of the produce for ourselves and sell any excess. During the harvest season, I work in our own fields. Some of the land is uncultivated wasteland and I often work there keeping the land clear. We have no pet animals, but we have one hen at home."

LIVING CONDITIONS IN INDIA

Housing is a problem for most of India's poor people. Millions of families have left their homes in rural India to find work in the cities. Here, they live in sprawling, makeshift, shanty towns or slums without proper drainage, sanitation or power. Some poor families live on the street with no shelter at all. In rural areas, homes are often built with baked earth bricks and plaster which easily crumble and collapse, especially in heavy rain. Most of India's poor live in overcrowded homes, which increases the spread of sickness and disease.

Children, scrounging for food or goods to sell, look through a garbage pile in a Calcutta slum in India.

Girls are more likely to be taken out of school (or have patchy attendance) because they are required to work or help with domestic chores.

LIFE FOR GIRLS IN INDIA

Girls in India are sometimes not valued as much as boys. This is partly because boys are considered to be capable of earning more money in the long term. In social terms, too, girls are often considered unequal in status. Some girl children are even aborted, or killed at birth. In general, girls receive far less education than boys, and in the Koppal district, the adult female literacy rate is just 27 per cent. In poor families, however, girls are just as likely to become child workers as boys – sometimes the work involves sexual exploitation.

"In our village there are Kurubas, Badigers, Naiks, Hajams, Bedas and Harijans (ethnic groups and castes). They are all Hindus. My family are Muslims. We are the only Muslims in our village. The best thing about my community (being a Muslim) *is going to a Mosque.*

Before I had to go to work, I went to school in the village. I started going to school when I was six years old. There were about 26 to 30 children in the school, but most of the children never used to come. There was only one room where classes from one to four were held. Later class five was added. There were two Sirs (teachers) at the school and lots of paintings. There were trees there, too.

The closest big town I have been to is Kanakgiri. Before I started going to work, I had never stepped out of my village. Last year, I visited the town of Koppal for my sister's marriage and I have been to the town of Gangawati. I did not see any children working in Gangawati. Adults work there – not children.

Would I like to go to other places when I am older? I would not go very far. I would go only to the nearest place and then come back. I fear going very far."

The children in Mehboob's village gather around, excited to be included in the photographs for the book.

The 'Dalits' rally sets off to march around India on December 6, 2003. The aim of the march was to increase awareness of the plight of the people considered 'impure' according to India's caste system. Paul Divakar (centre) is the leader of the National Campaign on Dalit Human Rights.

INDIA'S SOCIAL STRUCTURE

Most of India's population belong to the ancient Hindu faith. As with most faiths all over the world, a social structure emerged from the religion. It set out the society's rules, manners, and divisions of labour and importance. A large part of the structure was a class system, which in India is called the caste system. This system divided people up according to their occupation, which in turn defined their status. People belonging to the higher castes were generally quite well off, did not perform menial tasks, and were more respected and better educated. At the other end of the scale, were the lower or 'scheduled castes' as they are now known. These people often do not own land, and work as labourers or in other lower paid jobs. They are also known as 'Dalits', the 'oppressed' or 'untouchables'. Around 240 million people in India today are Dalits. The government's programmes for improving the lives of scheduled castes and small 'scheduled tribes' are not working quickly enough.

THE CASTE SYSTEM AND CHILD LABOUR

Access to education and loans to create a better life are very hard to come by for the scheduled castes. Although the caste system was abolished at India's independence in 1947, the old social structure that has lasted for thousands of years will take much longer to change. Education for the lower, or scheduled castes and small tribes is an important tool to help implement this change. In 2001, the Indian census included scheduled castes and tribes in its labour statistics.

"Before I went for work, I was studying in the 5th standard at school. After going for work, I never went back to school.

At school my favourite subject was Kannada. I can read and write Kannada and I received 96 per cent marks. I do not read books much. I have only read study books, but I read the newspapers. I liked social studies, too. In social studies I scored 35 per cent, in maths 26 per cent and in science 56 per cent. I also learned to make dishes for morning tiffin, like bajis, and I learned how to make tea. (Tiffin is a snack which is usually eaten with the fingers. Baji dishes are vegetables deep fried in batter.) At school, my sir's name was Kotresh. I liked to go to school, but my parents did not go to school, so I do not go now.

A teacher without a classroom in New Delhi, India. Over-population leaves schools under stress with poor facilities and often not enough teachers.

Mehboob works at his chores. Many parents feel that the education a child receives at school will not be relevant for the workplace.

Whenever I see children going to school, I feel like going, too. If I become a leader I will distribute play material to schools and make all children go to school!

I like music – all kinds of songs and cinema songs. (Mehboob sings one of the latest Kannada film songs for Kannan the interviewer. Mehboob has a good, rhythmic voice.)

I like to see movies, too. I see the movies on TV. There is no TV at my home, but I go to other people's houses to watch. Recently I have seen two Kannada films, 'Lady Tiger' and 'Naanobba Kalla' (I am a thief)."

EDUCATION IN INDIA

Some of India's schools are as fine as anywhere in the world, and they deliver top-quality education. But the pledge of compulsory education that is written in India's Constitution (see page 37) has not been enforced, and the level of education varies from state to state.

• There are not enough schools and teachers, and in some schools teachers do not turn up for days at a time. Children often have to travel a long way to school, especially at secondary level.

• Parents have to pay for books, clothes, equipment and travel expenses. These costs are often beyond the reach of poor families. India spends more money on secondary than primary education, so basic skills are not well taught in some areas.

• Education as a tool for change is not always appreciated. Parents feel that few of the jobs available to their children will require high levels of literacy and numeracy, so believe work-based training is all that is needed.

• Parents often feel that if the quality of school-based education or training is poor, it will not lead to more money in the future anyway.

• Statistics show that the children of child workers are more likely to become child workers themselves, while the children of educated parents are less likely to become involved in child labour.

"I had many friends in school. Two of my friends are Virupaksha and Hanumesh. Both of them still go to school. Virupaksha is in the 6th standard and Hanumesh is in class seven. There is no high school in our village, so they go to study in Metgal village. I meet my friends regularly and I still play with them. I met them this morning.

In school I used to play cricket and kabbadi. Now I play kabbadi in the evening in the village and in the school ground.

I enjoy playing games very much, but since I go to work, I don't get much time to play games.

Whenever I get free time, for example, at lunch break or when I come home, I still like to play.

When I am happy, I laugh. I feel happy when I am alone. Whenever I am alone I remember the times I spent with my friends and the joys during play.

I used to go to the mountains and hills with my friends. There is a mountain near my village. I would go to the mountain to collect firewood and also to play games with my friends. I saw bears and monkeys in the mountains. Now that I go to work at the agricultural farm, I do not go to the mountains any more."

Mehboob's disrupted social life is likely to leave him isolated, especially as his friends move on to secondary schools in other areas.

18

PLAYING KABBADI

Kabbadi is a 4,000-year-old game that tests strength and stamina. It is played on a court and players are divided into two teams of about 12 players each. Seven of each team's players take to the court at any one time. A player from each team enters the opponent's court in turn to be the 'catcher'. He tries to get his opponents 'out' by touching each of them – and gets a point for each one he touches. But while the catcher runs around he has to continually chant 'kabbadi', or in Mehboob's region, 'tho-tho-tho'. If the catcher is pulled down, or is too breathless to chant before he gets back to his own court, then he is out. The team with the most points wins.

Children in Mehboob's village play games. Kabbadi is a popular sport.

FREE TIME

Child workers are not given holidays or days off during the week as a right, and they are not paid for any free time. Their working day is normally extremely long – sometimes over 12 hours – so there is little time to play, socialise, take exercise or enjoy the countryside or entertainment. A minority of child workers is given a few rupees each week out of their wages. Most can only afford to buy a few sweets with this. Some go to the cinema, which is a favourite and cheap pastime in India. Girls might go shopping for accessories, such as inexpensive bangles.

The United Nation's 1989 treaty 'Convention on the Rights of the Child' states that all children (anywhere in the world) have the right to expect the time to enjoy play and recreation.

Child Worker – *Mehboob's Story*

"I am a Muslim, but I do not know much about the Muslims. We celebrate Ramzaan (Ramadan), *Bakrid and Muharram. I do not know why we celebrate Bakrid and Muharram. I do not know why we celebrate Ramzaan, but because it is God's day, we celebrate it.*

We are the only Muslim family in the village, so during the Ramzaan festival, I go to my uncle's house in Gangawati to celebrate. I get new clothes every year during Ramzaan. (Mehboob and his family celebrate the festival of Eid ul Fitr, which comes at the end of Ramadan.) *I wear the new clothes during the festival and that makes me happy. At Ramzaan, we prepare chicken dishes and biryaani* (rice dishes), *and we make sweets, such as mysore pakku, badushah and kesari bath.* (These sweets or small cakes are made from groundnut powder or wheat mixed with sugar and flavourings such as cashew nut.) *I like sweets. I like sweets very much!*

During Bakrid, community sharing is done. One sheep, or a goat, is bought and it is chopped up and the meat is shared among the contributors. At Muharram, we dig a pit and a fire is made in the pit. All the people gather around the fire pit, they move around it, they chant and they even play in the fire (sometimes men fence across the pit with fake swords).

When someone in the village dies, people cry and then he or she is taken to the graveyard and given a burial. Everyone in the village is buried in the same place, both Hindus and Muslims. The Hindus make the dead body sit up. When someone dies, he goes up to Paramatma (up to god).*"*

Muslims wait for the morning Eid prayer, at Jama Masjid mosque in Old Delhi.

THE POWER OF RELIGION

Religion is a powerful social and visual presence throughout India. From the country's vast cities to its tiny hamlets, sacred buildings, sculptures, images, performing arts and festivals reflect India's different faiths. All faiths teach peace and tolerance, but sometimes there can be religious conflict between India's different religious groups. Many children, like Mehboob, celebrate and take part in various religious festivals but do not necessarily study their faith.

Vendors sell goats to be sacrificed at the end of the Bakrid festival, which honours the offering of Prophet Abraham's son, Isaac, to God.

INDIA'S MAIN RELIGIOUS GROUPS

HINDUS 81.3% (of India's population): Hinduism is a set of ancient belief systems and deities rather than a centralised religion. It is one of the oldest faiths in the world. Its first writings, the Vedas, are about 3,500 years old.

MUSLIMS 12%: India first had contact with Islam only 80 years after the Holy Prophet Muhammad died in 632. Muslims follow the teachings in the Holy Qur'an.

CHRISTIANS 2.3%: St Thomas the Apostle is believed to have brought Christianity to southwest India about 54 years after the death of Jesus Christ.

SIKHS 1.9%: Sikhism was founded in the northwest region of Punjab by Sri Guru Nanak at the end of the 15th century.

OTHERS 2.5%: Including 5 million Buddhists. Buddhism began in India over 2,500 years ago. There are around 3.5 million followers of Jainism, around 90,000 Parsees, who follow the ancient faith of Zoroastrianism, and small communities of Jews living in India's main cities.

Hindus worship many gods. This is Ganesha, the elephant-headed god of wisdom and strength.

CHAPTER THREE: Going to Work

Across India, millions of children are going to work every day to enable their families to buy essentials, such as food. In many families like Mehboob's, the adults, who should be earning to support the family, have become ill and are no longer able to work. In addition to the lack of adult income, the families have to pay huge medical bills, leading to a never-ending spiral of poverty and debt. Along with 70 per cent of the world's working children, Mehboob primarily works in the agricultural sector.

All the working members of Mehboob's family work as agricultural labourers on seed farms. Between 1961 and 1991, the number of owner-farmers in India declined and the number of agricultural labourers, working for large, faceless companies, increased.

Like many working children, Mehboob does household chores as well as his 'real job'.

MEHBOOB SAYS ...

"I needed to work because my father was unwell and we have a large family, with younger brothers and sisters. My father does not go to work, so it is necessary for me to go to work and support the family.

My friends and other children from the village had gone to work before. They shared their experiences of working in seed-crossing with me and implored me to come with them. They told me that they got 25 rupees per day (30p). That got me interested!

At the time I started working, I had just completed the 5th standard (the final class in the village primary school) and was staying at home. When my friends shared their experiences of seed-crossing work with me, I felt like going, too. Money was definitely one of the criteria. I said to myself, they are earning money, why can't I do it? I was 8 years old when I started working."

CHILD LABOUR & DEBT

Millions of families in India live on low earnings or do not qualify for government financial support, so the only way to pay bills is to borrow money.

• Treatment for illness in India is not free. When a family member falls ill, the family has to pay for medical care.

• Living in poverty increases the risk of malnutrition and serious diseases, such as tuberculosis. This leads to a cycle of ill health, debt, poverty and, consequently, more ill health.

• Poor people take out loans to pay for healthcare, but do not have access to cheap loans. They often have to pay very high amounts of interest on a loan.

• Children work to pay off their parents' loans. Sometimes parents are paid an advance of money for their children's work. The children then work for nothing until the loan is paid back.

• Children often work as bondage. This means they are sent to work for the person who lent the parents money, instead of the money being paid back.

• Many children have to work to pay off debts they inherit from their parents when the parents die.

"I have had several jobs now. My first job was in a hotel. The hotel owner, Veerappa, had come to the village to enquire about children to work in his hotel. My father came to know about it and he agreed to send me for work. I went for work on my own, but it was on my father's insistence. I told my father that I want to go to school, but my father told me that he was unwell and I should go out to earn. Given a chance, I would go to school.

The hotel was a wayside dhaba, for tourists or business people (a hotel and eating place). I was taken by my father to the hotel in a bus. I was told the kind of work I would have to do – the owner had already explained to my father. I worked washing plates and utensils, and clearing tables. I would also serve food to the guests.

For six months I stayed away from home working at the hotel. I used to go home once in every 15 days, or once in a month, but I felt very bad about staying in the hotel. I always felt that I should have gone to school. I also felt bad that I was staying away from my parents."

Seven-year-old Indian child labourer, Haripada Maity, cleans dishes at a roadside food stall in Calcutta. Millions of children worldwide, especially girls, work 'behind the scenes' as domestic servants.

CHILD TRAFFICKERS

About two million children from poor families across the world are bought, sold, 'borrowed', kidnapped or lured away from their families every year. These young people are very often cheated or tricked into such situations by greedy family members, or by middlemen working for powerful syndicates. Many of these families are told that their children will have a better life away from home. Young teenage girls are promised marriages, which can turn out to be false or abusive.

The United Nations has identified some of the reasons why the trafficking of children takes place:

* to supply cheap, or even slave labour

* to provide workers for the sex industry

* to supply workers for domestic work

* to provide young girls as marriage partners.

Further investigation is also urgently needed into the trafficking of children for adoption and for body parts.

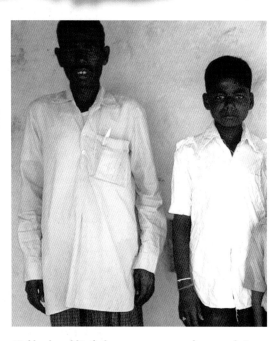

Mehboob and his father – some parents have no choice but to make their children work.

PARENT PRESSURE TO WORK

Child labour stems largely from poverty. But in studying the issue of child labour, it is also important to understand that the majority of child workers, work with the full knowledge and complicity of their parents. Some parents employ their own children in their workshops or fields because they feel they do not have to pay them. Poor parents are often deep in debt and need all family members to help them get out of it. Some parents are physically or mentally ill, or alcoholic, and cannot work. Whatever their situation, mothers and fathers around the world are forced by poverty to make the decision to take their children out of education and send them to work, often in dangerous environments far from home.

Child Worker – *Mehboob's Story*

"Whenever I made a mistake, the hotel owner would abuse me (verbally or by beating him). He would also complain to my father. I felt like going back home many times, but I could not go. My father had taken an advance of money and he also took my salary of 500 rupees in advance. I was forced to stay there in work.

I used to work from 5:30am to 10:00pm in the night. I was feeling bored, but still I had to do it. I remembered my school days and felt like I should have gone to school.

When my father was unwell he took an advance of 1,000 rupees, and so I had to work for two more months.

I used to sleep in the garage of the employer's house. The hotel was very near his home. I slept alone in the garage. I was given food by the hotel owner, but I like the food prepared by my mother and not by the owner. I got all kinds of food in the hotel, but there is no place like home. There is a mother in the home and she cooks with love."

Like any child or young person, Mehboob misses his family and home when he is forced to stay away at work.

CHILD WORKER WAGES IN INDIA

Many children receive no money at all for their work. This is because they are bonded labourers – they are working for someone who has given their parents a loan to pay off a debt. Some children do receive cash, but most of this has to be given straight to their parents. Typically, a child labourer working in a marble quarry might get paid about 15 rupees for a 10-hour working day. A cotton pollinator could earn 25 rupees for a 12-hour day at the height of the pollination season. In some parts of India this could buy, for example, about a dozen eggs. But it varies from job to job, region to region, and state to state.

Agricultural work, such as pollination on seed farms, is often seasonal and children are not paid for breaks in work.

Young children weave carpets in a workshop in Kashmir, India.

A GROWING DEBT

Family debt is a huge cause of child labour in India. The borrower not only has to pay back the loan, but also the cost of borrowing. That is, a percentage of the loan paid back regularly in interest. These interest rates are often extortionate (as high as 25 per cent) and mean that the actual amount of money owed never goes down and might never be repaid. As a result, it is impossible for some people to clear their debt with their child's employer. In these cases, the children are never paid a wage. Some employers also take away 'expenses' attached to employing the child. Again, this is added back on to the original loan.

CHAPTER FOUR: A Lost Childhood

The International Labour Organization (ILO) estimates that worldwide 180 million children are working in the worst forms of child labour: this includes 5.7 million forced into debt bondage or slavery, 1.8 million forced into prostitution or pornography and 300,000 recruited as child soldiers in armed conflicts. Millions more work day after day, month after month in hot, dusty, dangerous and sometimes poisonous environments.

MEHBOOB SAYS ...

"I left the hotel job for seed-crossing work. My father asked me to leave because seed-crossing was more money. Whenever seed-crossing work was not there (the work is seasonal), I went back to the hotel. I also went to work on a construction site, I worked in the paddy fields and I worked in a manganese ore mine in Hosepet. That was the most difficult job.

Priyanka, an Indian slum girl, breaks stones next to her siblings in the northeastern Indian city of Siliguri. Priyanka earns 150 rupees (£1.80) a week. She is three years old.

India is the world's biggest exporter of manganese ore, and the Karnataka region is a main source. The manganese is dug from open-cast mines.

We had to collect the lumps of manganese ore and break the stones and separate the manganese ore from the stone. The manganese ore lumps had to be segregated into big and small sized pieces. When I was working in the mines the conditions were not good. We had to work in the sun and my hands used to itch. Sometimes people would come in the night and steal the heaps you had segregated. I did not have any break from work except for taking food. I worked there for only 15 days and then someone came and told me that it was illegal mining that was going on there. So, I left the job in fear that I would be sent to jail."

THE DAMAGE & THE DANGERS

• Children working in light industry often have to sit in one position for hours at a time, causing bone distortion and cramped organs. Girls suffer damaged reproductive organs and pelvises, making childbirth difficult. Dim lighting in workshops can lead to poor eyesight.

• Quarrying, mining, construction, bricklaying and agricultural work involve heavy lifting and carrying, often on the head and in burning sun. Children suffer from chronic headaches and bent spines, leading to lameness.

• The above industries, together with gem polishing and textile work, produce enormous amounts of dust, which can lead to lung disease.

• Children often receive no meals or poor meals during their working day, leading to malnutrition and poor growth.

MINING FOR MANGANESE

Manganese powder is used to make steel, pesticides, fertilisers, batteries and some ceramics. But it is also a hazardous substance to the many child workers who mine the ore and are exposed to manganese dust. High levels of manganese attack the nervous system and lead to manganism. The symptoms are very similar to those suffered by people with Parkinson's disease and include fatigue, weakness, aching limbs, slow and clumsy movements and gradual crippling. Manganism is an incurable condition.

"When I was working in these places I used to think of school occasionally. But then I knew that the reality was that my father was ill. I expressed my desire to go to school to my mother, but she did not send me. She told me, 'Your father is ill and unable to work, there are a lot of children in the house and you should go out and earn.'

When I went for seed-crossing work, the employer came to collect us in a tractor. The tractor got a puncture and we went to Gangawati to repair it. The employer collects people and takes them to a camp and keeps them on the farm. My parents also came along with me during the camp and we lived in a temporary shed. For the past two years my father has not been well and therefore he does not come with us to camps.

I go to the camps when the employer contacts us. Now it is difficult to go to camp because my mother has to look after my father and my older sister has got married. I have never been to the camps alone.

The seed farm I work on is in a village called Metgal. The farm owner is in charge of the work. His name is Basawaraj.

Whenever he gets angry, he scolds or abuses. Not by beating, but by verbal abuse."

Mehboob works alongside other children at a seed farm. Employers are happy to employ children because there are so many of them available – if a child falls ill, they are easy to replace.

Children work inside an embroidery shop. Most child workers perform monotonous tasks that can lead to mental health problems through lack of stimulus.

Child brick makers move from construction site to construction site. Brick making entails carrying heavy clay and bricks in scorching, dusty conditions.

JOBS FIT FOR CHILDREN?

Most child labourers in India work in the agricultural sector. Others work in forestry, fishing, mining, construction and light industry. Agricultural work might include picking cotton, ploughing, looking after cattle, and taking care of and harvesting crops such as tea, coffee, tobacco, cashew nuts and cardamon. Some children pollinate crops. Children work in marble quarries, cutting and carrying marble slabs, or mining for poisonous manganese ore. Many children work in small workshops spending up to 15 hours a day rolling incense sticks, weaving carpets, and making items such as bangles, beedi (cigarettes) and matchsticks. Millions of girls work as domestic servants, many are abused and receive no payment.

CHILD WORKERS IN THE SEX TRADE

Child prostitution is a growing problem throughout the world, with children as young as six years involved. It is particularly rife in nations where millions live in poverty with poor access to education. Child traffickers force children into an organised sex trade, mostly in large cities. The children often receive no money of their own and cannot escape. Many never see their families again. The children suffer irreparable mental, physical and emotional damage and are open to sexually transmitted diseases such as HIV and AIDS, and unwanted pregnancies. The growth of tourism in poor countries has led to a boom in the trafficking of child sex workers to serve the tourist industry. Sometimes child soldiers are used by adult soldiers for sexual purposes.

"I work on the seed farm for several months at a time, working on the same half acre plot every day with some other children and adults. The flowers I work on are karela bittergourd. (Seed companies have agreements with farmers to buy all the seeds produced on the farmer's land.)

There is not much hardship in the work. The farmer ploughs the field and prepares the ground to sow the male and female plant seedlings. There are around 300 male seedlings, but a 1,000 female seedlings. When the seedlings grow, we are given a small chumta (tool) to cut open the male plant buds.

We collect the antrassu (pollen) from the bud. Then the pollen is dried overnight. Next day we are given the male powder in a ring pouch. Then the female plant buds are cut open, the petals are removed and only the stigma is kept. The stigma is dipped in the ring pouch to allow the female plant to mix with the male powder. This process continues for about one month. Each worker is allotted three rows. A lot of flowers are there and for each flower the same process is repeated.

First, the plant becomes a flower, then a fruit. When the fruit becomes ripe, it is cut open and the seeds are collected from that. Until that time the work is not over.

The seeds are then washed in acid and dried in the shade. After all the seeds have been collected from the plot, they are given to the seed company."

Mehboob works his way along a row of bittergourd, pollinating the plants using a ring pouch.

The bittergourd is considered very nutritious. It is also used in medicines.

SEED POLLINATION WORK

The bittergourd is a popular vegetable throughout South Asia and it is also exported. Karnataka state is one of the gourd's principal growers. However, the plant is prone to insect pests, such as fruit flies, and diseases such as watermelon mosaic virus and powdery mildew. Child workers pollinating, picking and pruning the gourds are often surrounded by hazardous chemicals. Mildew and other moulds are treated with sulphur dust, which child workers inhale. Sulphur dust affects breathing and irritates the eyes and skin.

COTTON FARMING

Cotton and cotton products are important exports for India, and Karnataka is a main producer. Hand pollination ensures good quality cotton and a more disease-resistant crop. Many children work 12-hour shifts at the height of the cotton-pollinating season. They become very expert in all areas of cotton growing. Most workers earn between 20 to 25 rupees per day. In a cotton-pollinator survey carried out in the Karnataka region in 2003–2004, there was a total number of 302 pollinators working. Of those, 203 were aged between 8 and 14. Skilled workers are often given advance wages to secure their labour for the whole season.

Cotton provides fibre for material and cotton wool. Oil, produced from its seeds, is used in both the food and pharmaceutical industries.

Child Worker – *Mehboob's Story*

"Once in a row, a boy cut down a plant. The boy implicated me and thinking that I had cut the plant, the owner abused me! There were three adults and three other children working in the plot. The names of the children were Yamnur, Sharanamma and Gangamma. All were around 10 years old.

On the farm I work from 6 am to 6 pm. The first break for food is at 9 am or 10 am for breakfast, then there is a break at 3 pm or 4 pm for lunch. The food is simple, roti, rice and daal. During this time we sleep at the farm. I now get 30 rupees per day for the seed-crossing work that I do. The money goes directly to my parents. Over the past three years, I have gone to the farm four or five times. When I'm not working on the seed farm, I go to the hotel. The seed-crossing job is the most easy for me, while working in the manganese ore mines was the most difficult.

When there is no work I stay at home without any problem. But if I want to play, no one is available as they have all gone to school. I like to play, but all my friends are in school. I know that children should not work and they should be going to school, but I am not sent to school. I know that

The UN's 1989 'Convention on the Rights of the Child' states that all children have the right to be protected from work that interferes with their education.

Mehboob lines up with the other workers at the seed farm for a meal break.

Nagaraj (a social worker from Plan, an organisation that helps children) has met my parents and asked them to send me to school. In front of him, they promise to send me to school, but they do not send me. I feel that sometimes I should leave all the work and go to school. Given a chance, I would definitely go to school.

My father has got cross with me many times in the past three years. Whenever I make any mistake, he gets cross. But I do not remember what mistakes I have committed. If he tells me to do something and I do not do it, or I forget to do it, he gets cross. But I like my father, even though he makes me work. I love my mother also. I love them both."

THE RIGHTS OF THE CHILD

In 1989, the United Nations amalgamated, for the first time, all the human rights standards that concern children in one single treaty, called the 'Convention on the Rights of the Child'. The complete list of rights in the convention is long, but these are the main points – regardless of race, colour, gender, religion, national or social origin, children have the right to:

- A name and a nationality.
- Express their thoughts, conscience and faith.
- Join organisations and take part in meetings.
- Privacy.
- Have access to information, including information about themselves.
- Adequate nutrition and medical care.
- Education.
- Full opportunity for play and recreation.
- Special care and equal opportunities if disabled in any way.
- Protection from abuse or neglect.
- Protection from dangerous drugs.
- Protection from sexual exploitation or being sold, abducted or trafficked.
- Protection from work that could be dangerous, harmful or inappropriate for the child's age.
- Defence, and respectful and appropriate treatment if accused of a crime.
- Protection in times of war. No child should be recruited into the armed forces under the age of 15.

Article 42 of the Convention establishes the right of all children to know about and understand the pledges made to them.

CHAPTER FIVE: Looking to the Future

Article 32 of the United Nation's 'Convention on the Rights of the Child' says: "States Parties recognize the right of the child to be protected from economic exploitation and from performing any work that is likely to be hazardous or to interfere with the child's education, or to be harmful to the child's health or physical, mental, spiritual, moral or social development." To date, 192 countries, including the United Kingdom and India, have signed and ratified this treaty.

MEHBOOB SAYS ...

"I want to become an agriculturist when I grow up, or I would like to live in a town, wear trousers and a shirt, and work in an office, because office work is easy.

I have not thought of how I would like to live when I grow up. I would like to have children, three children, and not make them work. I do not like adults who make children work.

First, I will send my children to school and after they grow up, I will send them to work. If they go to school, they will become intelligent and gain knowledge.

I am also intelligent. When you go to school you get knowledge and you develop your intellect. This ensures that you become a big man."

INDIA'S PROMISE

The Constitution of India was passed by the National Assembly in 1949, and came into effect in 1950. Its directives of state policy set out India's pledges and ambitions. The Constitution is the basis for law-making.

ARTICLE 23 of the directives establishes protection against exploitation, human trafficking and forced labour.

ARTICLE 24 prohibits the employment of children under 14 in factories, mines or in any other hazardous employment.

ARTICLE 43 pledges a living wage for all workers, conditions of work that ensure a decent standard of life, and full enjoyment of leisure.

ARTICLE 45 sets out its directive for free and compulsory education for all children up to the age of 14 by 1960. This still has not happened.

A young boy cleans shoes in a New Delhi street.

ILO CONVENTION NO. 138 (1973)

More commonly known as the 'Minimum Age Convention', the International Labour Organization's Convention No. 138 sets out clear guidelines for governments that define the minimum age at which children should be allowed to work in different types of employment in different countries. It states that children should complete their compulsory education before being allowed to work full time. It also sets out the minimum ages at which children should be allowed to do light work, such as household chores, and highlights jobs that children below a certain age should never be allowed to do, such as working during the night, and hazardous work such as mining.

CONVENTION ON WORST FORMS OF CHILD LABOUR

The ILO's Convention No. 182 (1999) was developed in order to respond to the challenges of some forms of child labour being so unacceptable that they need to be eliminated as quickly as possible. It is designed to tackle such intolerable situations as children being trafficked from country to country, children being forced to work in the sex trade, or as child soldiers, or in slavery.

Conventions No. 138 and No. 182 are complementary – they support one another. As well as getting rid of the worst forms of child labour, it is vital to keep in sight the ultimate goal of ridding the world of all forms of child labour.

KANNAN K. SAYS ...

"During my interview with Mehboob his childlike, deep desire to go to school was evident in his innocent talk. At the same time, Mehboob is also a young adult who realises that he needs to earn for his family. He also loves his father very much and cannot see him suffering – another reason why he readily agrees to go for work.

Mehboob takes his work seriously. In fact, during the interview, he described the process of working on the seed farm in such minute detail, that the social workers, translating the interview, could not re-translate some of the technical information.

Samuha-Plan have been making all efforts to send Mehboob back to school (Samuha is an organisation based in India which helps children and their families – Samuha works in partnership with Plan International). Nagaraj a social worker has made many visits to Mehboob's family and has suggested several options to help Mehboob continue his education, including having a private tutor at home – which the family cannot afford at present – or sending him to a night school. But to date, Nagaraj and others in Samuha-Plan have been unable to convince Mehboob's parents that the right place for this 13-year-old boy is in school. Mehboob's story clearly highlights the fact that child labour is both a consequence of poverty and a cause. Deprived of a good education, Mehboob's earning potential as an adult will be restricted. This will make it more likely that when he is grown-up, his own family will be poor, and perhaps Mehboob will have no choice but to send his own children to work. Wherever and whenever possible, Plan International tries to find a way to send children like Mehboob back to school. In Mehboob's case, as yet, there has been

Mehboob's deep yearning to go to school is common to many children in the area where Plan works.

no success. However, if the right conditions can be created, we hope one day Mehboob might go back to school.

It is important to realise that beatings, abuse and working in terrible conditions are not the only forms of suffering for child labourers. A lost childhood is also a cruel and sad thing for young workers like Mehboob."

A donation has been made to Plan UK for their involvement with this book. It will be used to help Mehboob and his community. Your contribution to Plan International can help many like Mehboob escape poverty and get back to school.
Contact Plan UK on: www.plan–uk.org

Will Mehboob's younger brothers and sister follow in his footsteps and soon go out to work?

A LOST CHILDHOOD
Will the cycle repeat itself? Will Mehboob's children have to work, too? Not if child workers' organisations can help it. 'Concerned for Working Children' is a worldwide child labour organization which set up a child workers' union in Karnataka. The union which is called Bhima Sangha, has 13,000 members and is a powerful supporter of working children. Bhima Sangha is aware that the principal cause of child labour is family poverty. So it aims to improve overall quality of life for parents and local communities, as well as improving working conditions for its members. Members of child labour organisations are keen to push for relevant education that, realistically for now, can be integrated into their working lives.

WHAT IS PLAN INTERNATIONAL?
The organisation 'Plan International' was set up over 60 years ago. It now provides opportunities for over a million children worldwide. Plan is currently working on around 5,000 projects in 45 of the world's poorest countries. Plan works with families and communities to improve children's lives through community projects that are financed by child sponsorship, government grants and corporate donations. Plan provides the funds and the skills, but it is the local community who implement and manage the projects.

Child Worker – *Mehboob's Story*

A BETTER FUTURE

Plan helps to improve living conditions for poor families and their children in India, by providing safe drinking water and sanitation facilities to rural and urban communities, by rebuilding or repairing homes that are unhealthy or dangerous, and by training farmers in agricultural techniques that will protect the environment and make the land more productive for many years to come.

HELPING FAMILIES TO HELP THEMSELVES

Plan helps families to form credit groups, so that they are able to access loans at nominal interest rates, in order to prevent them from falling into the clutches of unscrupulous, high interest money-lenders. They are also arranging vocational training programmes for young people and helping families start their own small businesses.

HELPING CHILDREN TO LEARN

Plan is working to improve education opportunities in India in many ways. They have set up day care centres for small children, enabling them to benefit from an early education; they are supplying books and equipment to schools, and to adolescents, lessening the financial burden on parents and encouraging more children to continue their studies beyond the primary level; and they are setting up education centres for young girls. In areas where few women can read and write, and girls are entered into child marriages, Plan runs camps where teenage girls can receive five years' worth of education in just six months.

HELP FOR THE KOPPAL DISTRICT

In the Koppal district of India, the International Water Management Institute and its partners are drawing up policies to make water more available and to tackle rural poverty. India's Gender and Health Equity Network and its partners are setting

In addition to reading, writing and mathematical skills, girls and young women learn about personal hygiene and other vital life skills at education camps.

up projects in Koppal to improve community healthcare awareness and practice, expand healthcare access and quality, and challenge public health providers to serve community needs.

HELPING PEOPLE WHO LIVE IN SLUMS

People living in the slums of Indian cities have often left the poverty of rural areas hoping to find a better life in the city. As the slums are illegal settlements, there is no basic infrastructure, such as sanitation facilities, clean water or drains. Families are vulnerable to disease, and the daily struggle to survive often means that attending school is not a priority for children. Drugs, alcohol abuse and HIV/AIDS are particular problems. Organisations like Plan work in slum areas to improve the sanitation and drainage, build roads,